BIG ENGLISH

2

2ND EDITION
STUDENT'S BOOK
with online resources

Contents

CLIL: Content and Culture	Phonics	Values	I can...
Math: Arithmetic plus, minus, equals 10 minus 6 equals... / 5 plus 5 equals... **Around the World: Classes** in a forest/garden, in the mountains, on a boat	**th** that, the, then, this, with bath, both, math, mouth, path, thin	**Take turns.** May I use the markers? It's your turn. Thanks.	...use words for classroom activities. ...use *there is*, *there are* to describe what's in my classroom. ...ask and answer about what people are doing in the classroom.
Science: Bones and muscles bone, jump, kick, move, muscle, throw We throw with our hands. When we jump, we use... muscles. **Around the World: Games** chase, dragon, freeze, join, move, shoulder, snake, tag	**ng, nk** bang, king, ring, sing, wing bank, ink, pink, sink, thank	**Play safely.** safe, seesaw, skateboard, slide, swing I'm safe on my skateboard. I always wear a helmet and pads.	...use words for outdoor activities. ...use round numbers 10–100. ...say what I like to do. ...say what people like to do.
History: At the museum burn, museum, new, oil, old, screen, wheel I think this is a computer. Really? I think it's a TV. **Around the World: Household objects** clay, comfortable, electricity, fridge, hammock, oven, pot, sand, solar	**oo** cool, food, moon, room, zoo book, cook, foot, good, look	**Be neat.** sink, toy box, washing machine	...use words for rooms of the house, furniture, and objects in the house. ...ask and answer about where things are.
Geography: Transportation around the world boat, canal, exercise, fast, ground, safe, slow, subway, without I use bikes and trains. Me, too! I don't use boats. **Around the World: Taxis** a long time ago, a lot of, colorful, modern, sign, special, wheel	**ai, oa** nail, rain, tail, train, wait boat, coat, oak, road, soap	**Cross the street safely.** cross, first, left, crosswalk, right, wait	...use words for places in town. ...use *want/wants to* + action words. ...say what I want to do. ...ask and answer about places in town.
Social Science: Goods and services carpenter, farmer, hairdresser, nurse, produce, provide, server, take care of **Around the World: Strange jobs** bicycle, canal, customer, lie, millions, push	**ar, er, or** arm, art, car, cart letter, singer, teacher born, corn, for	**Study hard and set goals.** art, math, music, science	...use job names. ...say what I want to be and why. ...ask and answer about what people want to be.
History: Telling the time burn, candle, cup, fall, height, hourglass, sand, shadow, sundial **Around the World: Different working hours** bakery, bread, fresh, market, store	**ch, tch, sh** chin, chop, lunch, rich match, watch, witch dish, fish, ship, she	**Be on time.** I get my backpack ready the night before school. I get up early on school days. I get dressed quickly and eat breakfast. I always get to school on time.	...use *o'clock* to tell the time. ...use the present simple to describe activities. ...talk about my daily routine with time expressions. ...ask and answer about daily routine activities.
Science: Healthy and unhealthy snacks candy, energy, fat, heart disease, label, potato chips, salt, snack, sugar, too much **Around the World: Where fruit comes from** avocado, beautiful, fabric, kiwi, leaves, pineapple, plants, popular, tropical, ugly, watermelon	**ee, ie** bee, cheese, feet, see, sheep cried, flies, lie, pie, tie	**Choose healthy foods.** apple, cookie, carrots, chips No chips for me, thanks. Just one cookie, please.	...use words for types of foods. ...use *like/likes* or *don't like/doesn't like* with food words. ...say what food I like and don't like. ...ask and answer about food people like and don't like.
Science: Animal habitats cover, desert, fox, jungle, lizard, ocean, raccoon, seal, whale **Around the World: Helping animals** camp, chimpanzee, elephant, feed, farm, horse, hurt, jungle	**ou, ow** group, soup, toucan, you clown, cow, down, owl, town	**Appreciate animals.** amazing, beautiful, smart, strong	...use words for wild animals. ...use *can/can't* with action words. ...ask and answer questions about what animals can do.
Geography: Celebrating special days celebration, confetti, hang, mask, pole, ribbon, wish In England, people celebrate May Day. May Day is in the spring. **Around the World: New Year's Eve** bell, chime, coal, luck, ring	**Alphabet**	**Be active all year.** fall, spring, summer, winter rake leaves, ride bikes, ice-skate, swim	...use words for months, seasons, and celebrations. ...use *always* or *never* to describe regular activities. ...talk about important activities and events that happen in a year. ...ask and answer questions about what people do at different times in a year.

1 Listen and read. Where is Jenny's backpack?

Welcome to Class!

2 Look at 1. Then match.

1 The pencil case is on the desk.

2 The notebook is on the shelf.

3 The book is on the chair.

4 The backpack is under Max.

a

b

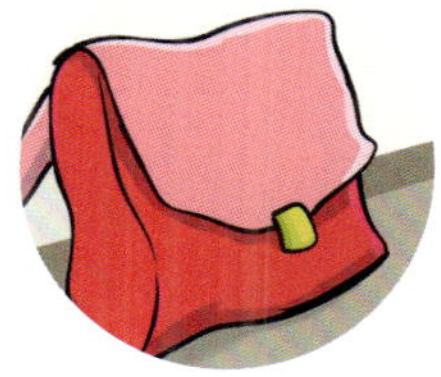

c

d

3 Look at 1. Read and circle.

1 Jamie is **combing his hair / taking a bath.**

2 Mom is **talking on the phone / eating.**

3 Dad is **drinking / making lunch.**

4 Max is **sleeping / playing.**

4 Act it out with a partner.

5 Listen, look, and write.

brother | Dad | Grandma | Grandpa | Max | Mom | sister

1 ____________

2 ____________

3 ____________

4 ____________

5 ____________

6 ____________

7 ____________

6 Look at 5. Read and match.

1 He has a book.
2 She has a phone.
3 He's sleeping.
4 She's eating.

a cat
b grandpa
c sister
d mom

7 Look at 5. Ask and answer.

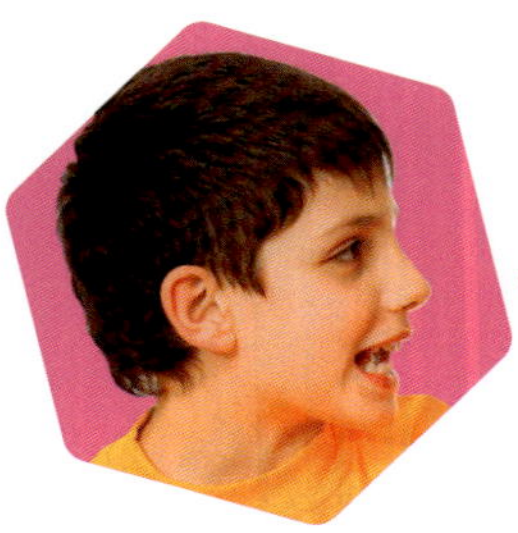

What's he doing?

Does she have a phone?

He's reading.

Yes, she does.

8 Look and read. Circle True or False. Listen and check.

6

1	The children are playing a game.	True	False
2	The markers are on the table.	True	False
3	The books are on the chair.	True	False
4	The pens are under the table.	True	False

9 Look at 8. Match.

1	Where is the pencil?	a	They're on the floor.
2	Where are the markers?	b	It's on the floor.
3	Where are the pencil cases?	c	They're on the table.

10 Look at 8. Ask and answer.

Where are the pens?

They're on the floor.

1 In My Classroom

Vocabulary

I will learn to name classroom activities.

7

Song Time!

8

1 Listen, look, and say.

1 coloring a picture

2 counting

3 cutting paper

4 gluing shapes

5 listening to a story

6 watching a movie

7 using the computer

8 writing her name

9 playing a game

2 Play the acting game.

I will learn to ask and answer about classroom activities.

3 Listen and sing. Then look at 1 and find.

10 11

Here's My Classroom!

Look! Here's my classroom.
And here are my friends!
Peter, Sarah, and Timothy,
Penny, Jack, and Jen!

Peter is cutting paper.
Penny is writing her name.
Sarah is listening to a story,
And Jack is playing a game.

Timothy is counting.
Jen is gluing.
We have fun and learn a lot.
What are your friends doing?

4 Listen and find in 1. Then say.

12

5 Look at 1. Ask and answer.

What's she doing?

She's coloring a picture.

THINK BIG What can we write? What can we count?

I will read a story about classroom activities.

14 **6** Listen and read. How many Marias are there?

What's Maria Doing?

7 Look at the story. Then match.

1 She's cutting paper.

2 She's gluing pictures.

3 She's using the computer.

4 She's writing on the board.

a

b

THINK BIG

Are there any girls called Maria in your class? How many?
How many children are there with the same name? What are the names?

Language in Action

I will listen to a dialog about classroom activities.

15

8 **Listen and read. Then say.**

Billy: What's Timmy doing?

Suzie: He's playing a computer game.

Billy: It looks like fun! Let's play a computer game, too.

Suzie: Sorry. There's only one computer.

Billy: Oh, too bad!

Suzie: But I have a DVD. Let's watch a movie!

9 **Look at 8. Role-play with a partner.**

16

10 **Listen and stick.**

11 **Look at 10 and write.**

1 There are ____________ new computers.

2 There are ____________ children in the class.

Grammar

I will learn to use *be* + *-ing* to describe what people are doing.
I will learn to use *there is*, *there are* + numbers.

What's he/she **doing**?	He'**s**/She'**s reading** a book.
What **are** they **doing**?	They'**re gluing** pictures.

he is = he's
she is = she's
they are = they're

17 12 Look and listen. Then write.

listening
playing
reading
writing

1 They're __________ soccer.

2 She's __________ a book.

3 They're __________ to music.

4 He's __________ numbers.

How many pictures are there?	**There's** one picture.
How many books are there?	**There are** three books.

there is = there's

18 13 Listen and write. Use There's or There are.

1 __________ one birthday cake.

2 __________ three shapes. 

3 __________ one big, black dog.

Content Connection | Math

I will learn to use math and numbers.

19 14 Do the math. Then listen and write.

1 Four plus three equals ________.
2 Eight minus two equals ________.
3 One plus nine equals ________.

CONTENT WORDS
plus +
minus –
equals =

20 15 Look, read, and write the answers. Then listen and check.

CONTENT WORDS
eleven 11 twelve 12 thirteen 13 fourteen 14 fifteen 15 sixteen 16
seventeen 17 eighteen 18 nineteen 19 twenty 20 thirty 30 forty 40
fifty 50 sixty 60 seventy 70 eighty 80 ninety 90 a hundred 100

1 There are eleven girls in the class and nineteen boys. There are ________ children in the class.

2 There are fourteen chairs in Classroom 1. The children move two chairs to Classroom 2. Now there are ________ chairs in Classroom 1.

3 The children have fifteen cupcakes. They eat four. Now they have ________ cupcakes.

4 There are eighteen pictures on the paper. Lucy cuts out two pictures. Now there are ________ pictures on the paper.

5 There are a hundred children on the playground. Thirty go into their classrooms. Now there are ________ children on the playground.

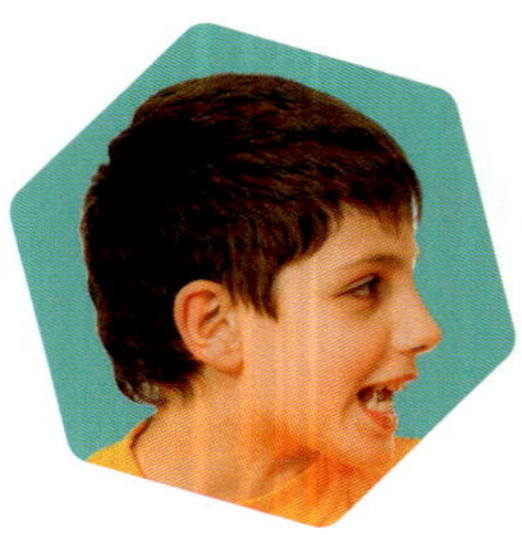

Eleven girls plus nineteen boys equals...

Thirty children!

THINK BIG When do adults use math?

I will learn about classrooms in different countries.

22

16 Look, listen, and read. What are they studying?

Classes, but Not in a Classroom!

Are classes always in classrooms?

No, they aren't!

1 These students in Turkey are in a forest. They're studying trees and animals.

2 These students in France are having a P.E. class in the mountains. They love to ski.

3 These students in the United States are having a science class in the school garden. They're growing plants and flowers.

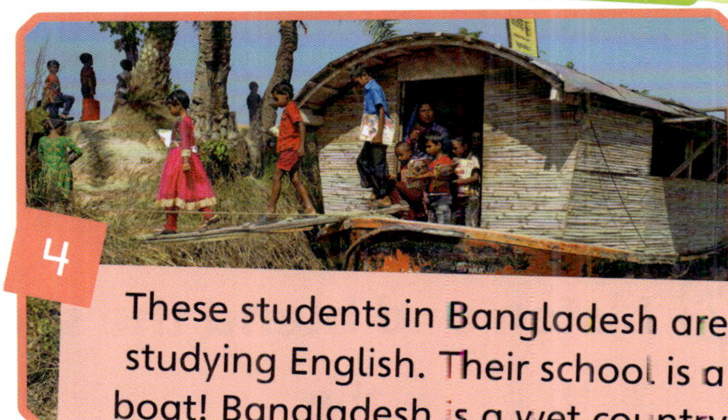

4 These students in Bangladesh are studying English. Their school is a boat! Bangladesh is a wet country. Sometimes schools close, but this school is always open.

17 Talk about your classroom with a partner.

Our classroom is in Mexico. There are twenty desks and chairs.

We have a big whiteboard and six new computers.

THINK BIG Do you have classes outside the classroom? Where do you go? What do you study?

Phonics | *th*

I will learn to use the sound *th*.

23

18 Listen, look, and repeat.

1 th   2 th

24

19 Listen and find. Then say.

bath

thin

this

that

25

20 Listen and blend the sounds.

1	th-e	the	2	th-e-n	then
3	b-o-th	both	4	w-i-th	with
5	p-a-th	path	6	m-a-th	math

26

21 Underline th and th. Then listen and chant.

There are three crocodiles
Taking a bath.
They have thin mouths,
But big teeth!
Look out! Look out!

I will learn to talk about taking turns.

28

22 Listen and look. Number in order.

23 Take turns. Ask and answer with a partner. Do the actions.

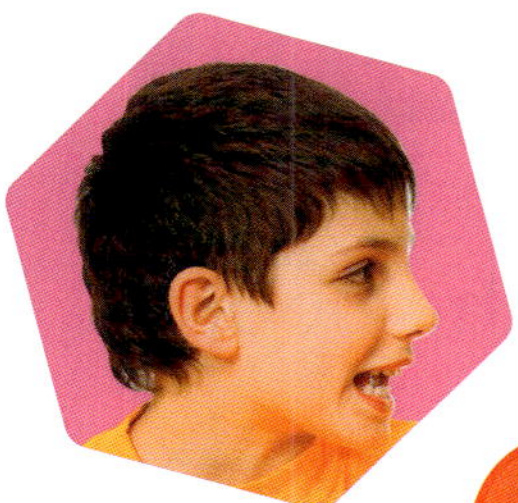

May I use the computer now?

Yes! Let's take turns.

THINK BIG Is it good to take turns? Why?

Project

24 Make a finger puppet. With a partner, use your puppet to do a role play about taking turns.

25 Look and write. Use the correct form of the verb.

color glue listen play read write

1 She's ________ shapes.

2 They're ________ a book.

3 They're ________ to music.

4 They're ________ soccer.

5 She's ________ a picture.

6 He's ________ on the board.

26 Count and write. Use There's or There are.

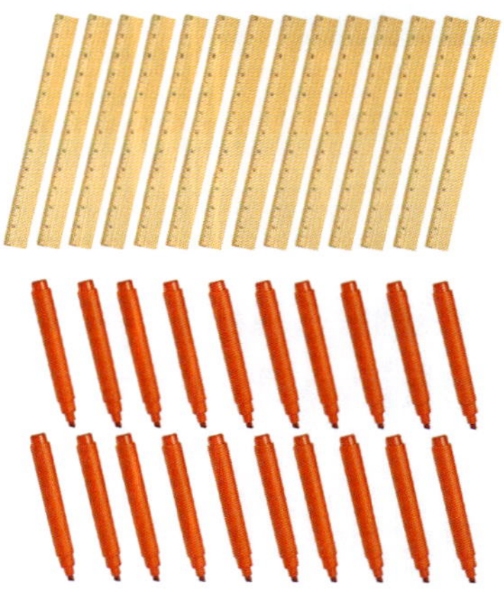

1 ________________

________ rulers.

2 ________________

________ eraser.

3 ________________

________ markers.

I Can

- use words for classroom activities.
- use *there is*, *there are* to describe what's in my classroom.

29
27 **Listen and find. Say Picture 1 or Picture 2. Then ask and answer.**

Picture 1

Picture 2

In Picture 1, what are they doing?

In Picture 1, they're playing a game.

I Can

- ask and answer about what people are doing in the classroom.

2 My Games

Vocabulary

I will learn to name outdoor activities.

30

Song Time!

31

1 Listen, look, and say.

1 play basketball

2 play volleyball

3 play baseball

4 play on the slide

5 kick a soccer ball

6 skate

7 skateboard

8 ride my bike

2 Play the acting game.

Song

I will learn to ask and answer about outdoor activities.

3 Listen and sing. Then look at 1 and find.

32 33

Come On and Play

We're playing on the playground.
There are lots of games to play.
Soccer, baseball, and basketball.
What do you want to play today?

Paul likes to play on the swings.
Vera likes to play on the slide.
We all like to play hide-and-seek.
Are you ready to run and hide?

We're playing on the playground.
It's always so much fun.
Come on and play with us.
We play with everyone!

4 Listen and find in 1. Then say.

34

5 Look at 1. Ask and answer.

I like to play volleyball.

Picture 2.

THINK BIG

What games can children play on the playground?
What games can children play in the classroom?

I will read a story about outdoor activities.

36

6 Listen and read. What does Jenny like to do?

We Like to Play Together!

7 Look at the story. Then circle.

1  likes to **play soccer** / **ride his bike**.

2  likes to **play baseball** / **skateboard**.

3  likes to **play volleyball** / **play basketball**.

THINK BIG

What do you like to play on the playground?
What team games do you know?
Do you like to play on a team? Why?

I will listen to a dialog about outdoor activities.

37 8 Listen and read. Then say.

Len:	I like to play with Ted and Judy. They're fun!
Betty:	What do they like to do?
Len:	They like to play hide-and-seek.
Betty:	I like to play hide-and-seek, too!
Len:	Great. Let's play!

9 Look at 8. Role-play with a partner.

38 10 Listen and stick.

Grammar

I will learn to use *like to* + verb to describe what people like to do.
I will learn to use *between*, *behind*, *in front of*, and *next to*.

What **does** he/she **like to do**?	He/She **likes to skate**.
What **do** they **like to do**?	They **like to play basketball.**

40

11 Listen and write. Then say.

1 What ____________ Matt like to do?
He ____________ listen to music.

2 What ____________ Becky and Ron like to do?
They ____________ play video games.

3 What ____________ she like to do?
She ____________ ride her bike.

41

12 Listen and write the words.

between behind in front of next to

1 It's ____________ the slide.

2 It's ____________ the seesaws.

3 It's ____________ the bat.

4 They're ____________ the swing.

I will learn about muscles and bones in the body.

42 13 Look and listen. Say the numbers.

13 26 27 34 70

43 14 Listen and read. Write the numbers.

CONTENT WORDS
bone jump kick move muscle throw

Playing is fun. When we move, we use our bones and muscles. Bones and muscles help us play.

We throw with our hands. Our hands have many bones. One hand has ______ bones.

We kick with our feet. Our feet have many bones, too. One foot has ______ bones.

When we throw a ball, we use ______ muscles.
When we kick a ball, we use ______ muscles.
When we jump, we use more than ______ muscles.

We need to take good care of our bones and muscles.

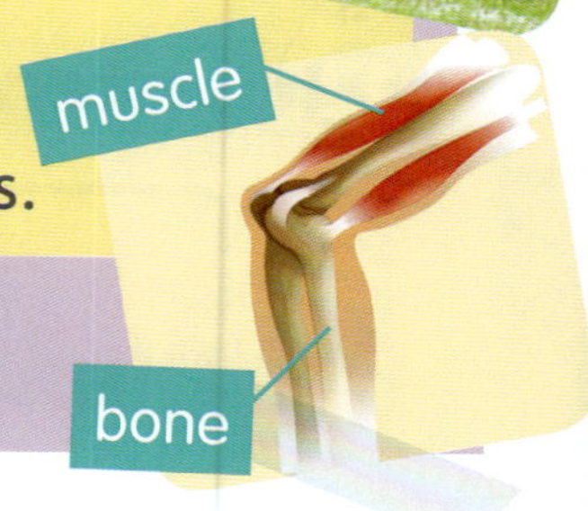

15 Look at 14. Read and match.

1 Bones and muscles
2 Our feet
3 When we throw a ball, we
4 When we jump, we

a use more than 70 muscles.
b help us play.
c have a lot of bones.
d use our hands.

THINK BIG

Which activities use our muscles the most?
dancing using a computer watching movies
playing basketball riding a bike

Culture Connection | Around the World

I will learn about games played in different countries.

16 **Look at the pictures. Which games do you know?**

CONTENT WORDS

chase dragon freeze join
move shoulder snake tag

Tag! You're It!

1 In Ghana, Africa, children play Big Snake. One child is the "snake." The snake runs and tags another child. That child holds the snake's hand. Together they try to tag other children. Other children join the snake. At the end, there is one very big snake!

2 In Mexico, children play Sun and Ice. There are two teams. On each team, one child chases and tags a child on the other team. That child must freeze. He or she can't move. If another person on that child's team touches the child and says "Sun!", the child can move again.

3 In China, children play Catch the Dragon's Tail. Children stand in a line. They put their hands on the shoulders of the child in front of them. This is the "dragon." The first child is the head of the dragon. The last child is the tail. The head chases the tail. If the head child tags the tail child, the head child becomes the tail. A new child becomes the head. It's even more fun with two dragons!

45

17 **Listen and read. Then match with the pictures.**

THINK BIG What "tag" games do you know? How do you play them?

Phonics | *ng, nk*

I will learn to use the sounds *ng* and *nk*.

46 18 Listen, look, and repeat.

1 ng 2 nk

47 19 Listen and find. Then say.

ring

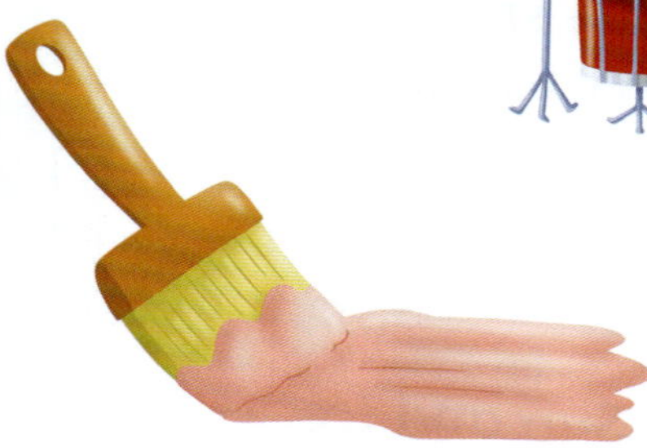

pink

bang

ink

48 20 Listen and blend the sounds.

1	k-i-ng	king	2	w-i-ng	wing
3	th-a-nk	thank	4	s-i-ng	sing
5	b-a-nk	bank	6	s-i-nk	sink

49 21 Underline ng and nk. Then listen and chant.

Sing a song about a king.
Thank you! Thank you!
He has a big, pink ring
And big, blue wings.
Thank you! Thank you!

Values | Play safely.

I will learn to talk about playing safely.

51

22 Look, listen, and number. Then say.

I'm safe on my skateboard. I always wear a helmet and pads.

I'm safe on the swing. I always sit down.

We are safe on the seesaw. We put one leg on each side.

I'm safe on the slide. I always keep my feet in front of me.

THINK BIG

Do you play safely? How?

Project

23 Make a Playground Safety checklist. Check (✓) what you do.

Playground Activities	Safety Tips	I Play Safely
seesaw	put one leg on each side	✓
slide	keep feet in front of you	
swings	don't stand up	
skating	wear knee pads	
bike riding	wear a helmet	

24 Look and write.

1 He ________________ to play on the slide.

2 They like to ________________.

3 She likes to ________________ soccer.

4 ________________ to play baseball.

25 Look and write.

behind	between	in front of	next to

1 The boy is hiding ____________ the tree.

2 The girl is standing ____________ the slide.

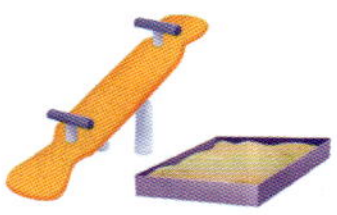

3 The sandbox is ____________ the seesaw.

4 The girl is standing ____________ the swings.

26 Read. Write the numbers.

1 twenty-nine ______ 2 fifty ______ 3 forty-six ______

4 one hundred ______ 5 sixty ______ 6 seventy ______

I Can

- use words for outdoor activities.
- use *behind, between, in front of,* and *next to.*

27 Work in groups. Play the Memory game.

Student 1:
What do you like to do on the playground? Say.

Student 2:
Talk about Student 1. What does she like to do? Then say and act out what you like to do.

Student 3:
Talk about Students 1 and 2. Then say and act out what you like to do.

Play with your group. Can you remember what everyone likes to do?

I Can

- say what I like to do.
- say what people like to do.

3 In My House

Vocabulary

I will learn to name rooms and furniture.

53

Song Time!

54

1 Listen, look, and say.

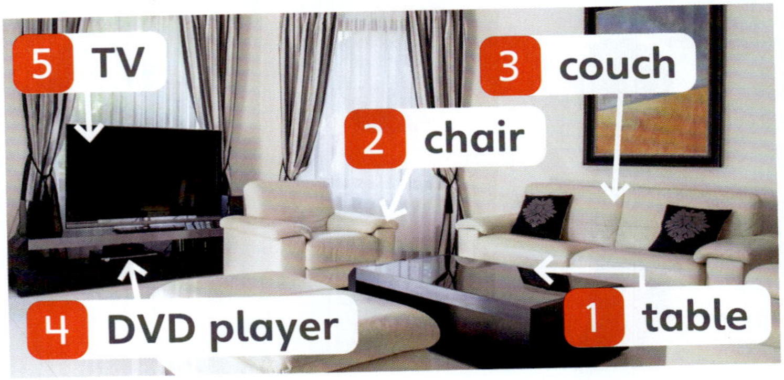

living room

bathroom

kitchen

bedroom

2 Play the *I Spy* game.

Song

I will learn to ask and answer about rooms and furniture.

55 56

3 **Listen and sing. Then look at 1 and find.**

Where Are My Keys?

Where are my keys, Mom?
Your keys are on the chair.
The chair? Which chair?
There are chairs everywhere!

There's a chair in the living room
And one in the bedroom, too.
There are chairs in the dining room.
I don't know which chair. Do you?

Your keys are where you left them.
Put on your glasses and see.
They're on the chair behind you.
My keys are there! Silly me!

57

4 **Listen and look at 1. Say yes or no.**

5 **Look at 1. Ask and answer.**

Where's the bathtub?

It's in the bathroom.

THINK BIG

What rooms in your house do you use for washing?
What rooms in your house do you use for eating?

I will read a story about family and home.

59

6 **Listen and read. How many cousins does Jamie have?**

A Family Visit

7 Look and write.

bedroom living room kitchen

1  Jamie's cousins are in the ________________.

2  Now they're in Jamie's ________________.

3  The TV is in the ________________.

THINK BIG

Who are they?
My father's brother is my…
My father's sister is my…
My uncle's son is my…

Language in Action

I will listen to a dialog about where things are.

60

8 Listen and read. Then say.

Mom: Michael, where are my keys?

Michael: They're on the table next to your cup.

Mom: Thanks. Where's my phone?

Michael: It's in Emily's room.

Mom: Why is it in your sister's room?

Michael: She's texting her friends.

Mom: Emily!

9 Look at 8. Role-play with a partner.

61

10 Listen and stick.

Grammar

I will learn to use *it's* and *they're* to describe where things are.
I will learn to use name +*'s* to describe who things belong to.

Where**'s** the TV?	**It's** on the table.
Where **are** the chairs?	**They're** in the living room.

11 Write It's or They're.

1 Where's the computer? ______________ in the living room.

2 Where's my jacket? ______________ in the closet.

3 Where are my glasses? ______________ on the table.

4 Where's the dresser? ______________ next to the bed.

My mother**'s** phone is on the dresser.
Ben**'s** keys are on the table.

12 Write. Use the names.

1 Where's ______________ backpack? (Hannah)

2 I see ______________ phone. It's next to the TV. (Dylan)

3 ______________ jacket is in the closet. (Joe)

4 Your ______________ homework is on his bed. (brother)

5 My ______________ games are fun! (grandma)

13 Work with a partner. Ask and answer.

Where's Manny's pencil?

It's under his desk.

I will learn about old and new things.

14 Look at the pictures. What are they? Talk with a partner.

a 

bike computer lamp TV

b 

c 

I think Picture b is a computer.

Really? I think it's a TV.

d 

15 Look, read, and circle. Then listen and check.

63

CONTENT WORDS
burn museum new
oil old screen wheel

Emma White

At the Museum

1 Do you like museums? I do! My favorite museum is the Science Museum. I love the old things there. There are some very old **wheels** / **lamps** at the museum. They're 2,000 years old. They need oil in them. The oil burns.

2 There's an old **computer** / **screen** at the museum, too. You can put a new computer in a backpack, but this computer needs a big room.

3 This old **bike** / **TV** is very funny. It's big, but the screen is small.

4 My favorite thing at the museum is an old **lamp** / **bike**. One of its wheels is very big, and one wheel is very small. When you ride it, you sit on the big wheel. It's great!

THINK BIG Name one old thing and one new thing in your classroom and home.

Culture Connection | Around the World

I will learn about objects people use at home around the world.

CONTENT WORDS

clay comfortable electricity fridge hammock oven pot sand solar

65

16 Look, listen, and read.

Household Objects

1 In Sudan, some people keep their food cold in clay pots. They put one pot in another, with wet sand between them. A fridge needs electricity, but these pots don't. They can keep food cold anywhere.

2 Some people in Mali cook with a solar oven. A solar oven uses the sun. When this oven is in the sun, it's very hot, and it cooks the food quickly.

3 Do you like these chairs? This is a restaurant in Japan. The chairs don't have legs, but they're comfortable.

4 Some people in Sarawak, Malaysia, sleep in hammocks. They don't use beds. The hammocks are very comfortable.

17 Look at 16. Find the words. Then write.

At home, we keep food cold in a ¹____________. When we cook food, we use an ²____________. When we eat dinner, we sit on ³____________s. We sleep in ⁴____________s.

THINK BIG Do you want the things in the pictures in your home? Why/Why not?

Phonics | oo

I will learn to use the sound *oo*.

66
18 Listen, look, and repeat.

1 oo 2 oo

67
19 Listen and find. Then say.

moon

book

zoo

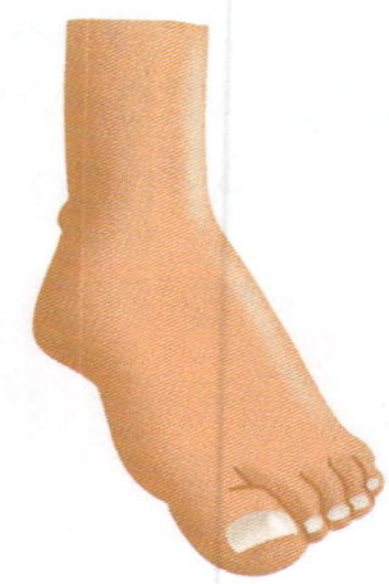

foot

68
20 Listen and blend the sounds.

1	r-oo-m	room	2	l-oo-k	look
3	f-oo-d	food	4	c-oo-k	cook
5	c-oo-l	cool	6	g-oo-d	good

69
21 Underline oo and oo. Then listen and chant.

Look in my cookbook.
The food is good!
The food is cool!

I will learn to talk about being neat.

22 Listen and write. Then say.

71

sink | toy box | washing machine

1 I put my toys in the ______________________.

2 I put my dirty dishes in the ______________________.

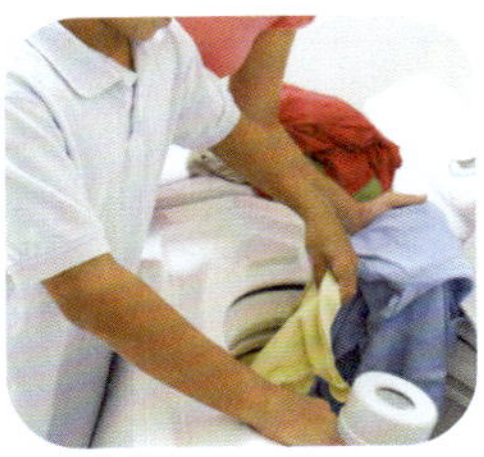

3 I put my dirty clothes in the ______________________.

23 How do you keep your home neat? Act it out. Your partner guesses.

THINK BIG Is it good to be neat at home? Why?
Is it good to be neat in class? Why?

Project

24 Make your own Toy Box.

1 Cut.

2 Tape.

3 Write.

25 Look and write.

bathtub chair dresser fridge lamp oven

1 ______________ 2 ______________ 3 ______________

4 ______________ 5 ______________ 6 ______________

26 Read and write.

are in on sunglasses Tina's where's

Donny: Sara, ______________ my math book?

Sara: It's ______________ the dining room ______________ the table.

Donny: Thanks. Hey, ______________ those your ______________?

Sara: No, they're ______________ sunglasses.

Donny: They're cool.

I Can

- use words for rooms of the house, furniture, and objects in the house.

27 Look. Choose a room for each thing. Draw a line.

keys

phone

soccer ball

glasses

roller skates

hat

28 Look at 27. Ask and answer.

Where are the keys?

They're on the table in front of the bed.

I Can

- ask and answer about where things are.

Do I know it?

1 Think about it. Look and circle. Practice.

I know this.

I need more practice.

I don't know this.

1 p. 4

2 p. 16

3 p. 28

4 p. 28

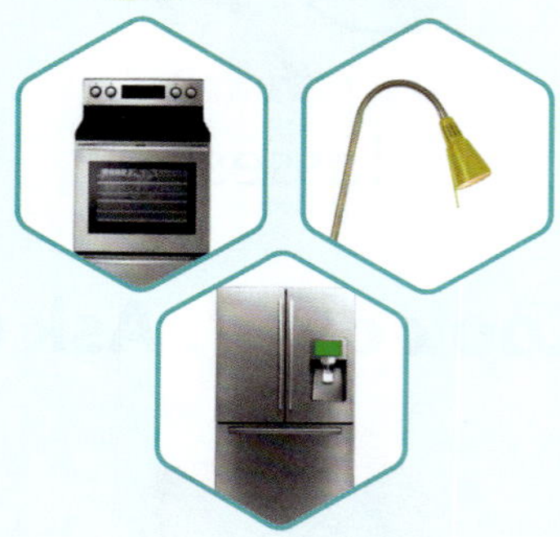

5	What's he doing? He's reading a book.	p. 9
6	How many computers are there? There's one computer./There are three computers.	p. 9
7	What do they like to do? They like to skate.	p. 21
8	Where's the table? It's in the kitchen.	p. 33

Have students review the key language. Go to the pages indicated in each box.

I can do it!

73

2 Get ready.

A. Look, listen, and write.

between on under

Miss Davis: What's your favorite game on the playground?

Beth: I like to play soccer.

Adam: I like to play [1]____________ the swings.

Katy: And I like to skate!

Miss Davis: OK. Where's the soccer ball?

Beth: It's [2]____________ the chair.

Miss Davis: And where are Katy's skates?

Adam: They're [3]____________ the two chairs.

Miss Davis: OK, everybody. Take your things and go outside. And be quick!

B. Look at **A** and point. Ask and answer with a partner.

What's he doing?

He's coloring a picture.

C. Look at **A**. Point and say how many. Use **There's** or **There are**.

chairs soccer ball teacher

3 Get set.

Cut out the cards on page 133.
Now you're ready to **Go**!

74 4 Go!

A. Look at the cards and write. Listen and check.

are	coloring	on	reading	they're	under

1 In pictures 1 and 2, they're ____________ a picture.
2 In pictures 3 and 4, ____________ playing soccer.
3 In pictures 1 and 3, they're ____________ a book.
4 In pictures 2 and 4, there's a basketball ____________ the table.
5 In pictures 1, 2, 3, and 4, there ____________ keys ____________ the table.

B. Point to a card. Ask and answer with a partner.

What do they like to do?

They like to play soccer.

Where are the keys?

They're on the table.

5 Write or draw.

All About Me

What do you like to do in your classroom?	Where do you like to read?
What do you like to do on the playground?	Where are your toys?

Do I know it now?

6 Think about it.

A. Go to page 40. Look and circle again.

B. Check (✔).

- ☐ I can start the next unit.
- ☐ I can ask my teacher for help and then start the next unit.
- ☐ I can practice and then start the next unit.

7 Rate this Checkpoint. Color.

hard OK easy | not fun OK fun

4 In My Town

Vocabulary

I will learn to name places in town.

75

Song Time!

76

1 Listen, look, and say.

1 movie theater

2 gas station

3 restaurant

4 train station

5 bus stop

6 post office

7 bookstore

8 computer store

9 supermarket

10 shopping mall

11 bank

2 Play the memory game.

Song

I will learn to ask and answer about places in town.

77 78

3 Listen and sing. Then look at 1 and find.

Maps Are Great!

Where's the bookstore?
I want to buy a book.
Here, I have a map.
Come on. Let's take a look!

The bookstore is on River Street.
It isn't far from us.
Do you want to walk there?
No, thanks! Let's take the bus!

I want to mail a letter, too.
Is there a post office?
Do you know?
I'm looking at the map.
Yes, there is.
It's near the bookstore.
Come on. Let's go.

Maps are really great.
I use them every day.
In town or out of town,
They help me find my way!

79

4 Listen and number.

5 Look at 4. Ask and answer.

Where's the restaurant?

It's on Castle Road. It's next to the gas station.

THINK BIG

What can you see at a bus stop?
What can you eat in a restaurant?

I will read a story about different places.

81

6 **Listen and read. Where are Jenny and her dad?**

Is There a Bookstore?

7 Look and read. Write.

1 Jenny's dad wants to buy a book at the ________________.

2 Jenny wants to buy a ________________ ________________ at the computer store.

3 Jenny and her dad want to eat lunch at a ________________.

4 Jenny wants pizza and ________________.

5 Dad doesn't have his ________________.

THINK BIG Do you like to shop? Where do you go shopping? What's your favorite store? What do you buy?

I will listen to a dialog about places and directions.

82 8 Listen and read. Then say.

Julie: What do you want to do today, Aunt Anna?

Aunt Anna: I want to mail some postcards. Is there a post office near your house?

Julie: No, there isn't. There's one on Market Street.

Aunt Anna: Market Street? That's far, isn't it? Is there a bus stop near here?

Julie: Yes, there is.

Aunt Anna: Great! Let's go!

9 Look at 8. Role-play with a partner.

83 10 Listen and stick.

Grammar

I will learn to use *want/wants to.*
I will learn to use *Is there* and *There is/isn't.*

I/We/They/You **want to** mail a letter.	He/She **wants to** go to the park.

11 Write want to or wants to.

1 Mom __________ put gas in the car.
2 I __________ buy a book.
3 My brother and I __________ eat pizza for lunch.
4 Paula and Rick __________ see a movie.

Is there a post office near here?	Yes, **there is**.
Is there a bank on Elm Street?	No, **there isn't**.

12 Look at the map on page 48. Write answers.

1 Is there a bank on Cherry Street? Yes, there is.
2 Is there a train station on Market Street? __________.
3 Is there a gas station on Maple Road? __________.
4 Is there a café near the computer store? __________.
5 Is there a bus stop on Elm Road? __________.

13 Ask and answer. Use the sentences in 12 and the map on page 48.

Is there a bank near here?

Yes, there is. It's on Cherry Street.

Content Connection | Geography

I will learn about transportation.

85 **14** **Look, listen, and read. Then match and write a–d.**

CONTENT WORDS
boat canal exercise fast ground
safe slow subway without

How Do You Go to School?

1 I live in Bangkok, and I go to school by boat. There are a lot of canals here, and there are a lot of boats on the canals. ☐

Sunan

2 Here in Mexico City, there are a lot of cars on the streets. Going by car is slow. I always go to school by bus. It's fast, and the bus stop is near my school. ☐

Carmen

3 I go to school by subway train. It goes under the ground. There are a lot of subway trains here in New York, and there are 468 stations! One of the stations is very close to our apartment. ☐

Sophia

4 I live in Amsterdam, and I go to school by bike. My friends ride their bikes, too. There are a lot of "bike streets" here – streets without cars. They're safe, and it's good exercise. ☐

Lars

15 **Do a class survey. Ask and answer.**

	bus	train	boat	bike	other
Sam	✓				

Sam, how do you go to school?

I go to school by bus.

THINK BIG What other ways can you use to go to school? Are they fast or slow?

I will learn about taxis around the world.

16 Look at the pictures. What kind of car do they show?

CONTENT WORDS
a long time ago · a lot of · colorful · modern · sign · special · wheel

Taxi!

There are taxis in every city in the world, but they aren't all the same.

1 In London, most of the taxis are big and black. They are new and modern, but they look like cars from a long time ago.

2 In Berlin, taxis aren't very colorful. They're very light brown, with a black and yellow taxi sign on top.

3 In New Delhi, a lot of taxis have only three wheels! They're green and yellow, and they have a special name: tuk tuk.

4 In Havana, there are a lot of colorful taxis. These black and yellow taxis have three wheels. They're modern and really fun.

a

b

c

d

87

17 Listen and read. Then match and write 1–4.

THINK BIG Why do people take taxis? Which taxi in the pictures do you like? Why?

I will learn to use the sounds *ai* and *oa*.

88 18 Listen, look, and repeat.

1 ai   2 oa

89 19 Listen and find. Then say.

train

rain

boat

coat

90 20 Listen and blend the sounds.

1	n-ai-l	nail	2	oa-k	oak
3	t-ai-l	tail	4	s-oa-p	soap
5	w-ai-t	wait	6	r-oa-d	road

91 21 Underline ai and oa. Then listen and chant.

Wear a coat
To sail the boat!
Drive the train
In the rain!

Values | Cross the street safely.

I will learn how to cross the street safely.

93

22 Listen and write. Then say.

cross look wait

1 First, I always ______ at the crosswalk.

2 Second, I ______ for the green man.

3 Last, I ______ left, then right, then left again before I cross the street.

THINK BIG What animal does a crosswalk look like? Does a crosswalk always have lights? Find out.

Project

23 Make a Cross Safely poster.

24 Read and match.

1 I want to buy a book.

2 Tim wants to see a movie.

3 Mom and Dad want to put gas in the car.

4 Ben wants to send a letter.

a There's a movie theater near the bus stop.

b There's a post office on Main Street.

c There's a bookstore on Maple Road.

d There's a gas station next to the bank.

25 Look and write. Use by.

1 Many children go to school ____________.

2 My sister comes home ____________.

3 My mom goes to the bank ____________.

26 Read and circle.

Maria: Dad **want to** / **wants to** eat Chinese food for lunch. But I **want to** / **wants to** eat Mexican food.

Mom: **There is** / **Is there** a Chinese restaurant near here?

Bill: Yes, **there is** / **there isn't**. Let's go there.

I Can

- use words for places in town.
- use *want/wants to* + action words.

27 Work in two groups. Make sentence cards.

Group A:

Write sentences starting with *I want to*. Write a different activity for each student in the group.

Group B:

Write sentences starting with *There's a*. Write a different place for each student in the group.

28 Groups A and B: Take turns reading your cards. Find your match.

I want to buy a book.

Yes, a match!

There's a bookstore near here.

I Can

- say what I want to do.
- ask and answer about places in town.

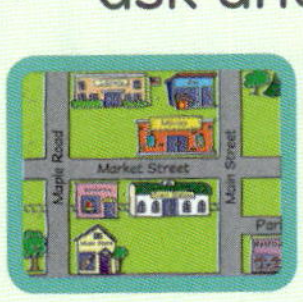

5 My Dream Job

Vocabulary

I will learn to name jobs.

94

Song Time!

95

1 Listen, look, and say.

1 actor

2 artist

3 dancer

4 doctor

5 writer

6 pilot

7 singer

8 athlete

9 teacher

10 chef

11 vet

2 Play the acting game.

I will learn to ask and answer about jobs.

96 97

3 Listen and sing. Then look at 1 and find.

Hey, What Do You Want to Be?

Hey, what do you want to be?
You have to choose just one.
There are so many different jobs.
I want one that is fun!

I want to be a dancer
And an athlete, too.
Or maybe a teacher.
What about you?

I want to be an actor,
And I want to be a vet.
I want to be a pilot, too.
Then I can fly a jet!

Chorus

98

4 Listen and write.

1 I want to be a ____________.

2 I want to be a ____________.

3 I want to be a ____________.

5 Look at 1. Ask and answer.

What do you want to be?

I want to be a chef.

THINK BIG

What jobs do people do at your school?
What jobs do people do in your town?

Story

I will read a story about jobs.

100

6 **Listen and read. What does Jamie like to do?**

Dream Jobs!

7 Look at the story. Write.

1 Jenny wants to be a ______________________.

She likes to ______________________.

2 Dan wants to be a ______________________.

He likes to ______________________ stories.

3 Maria wants to be a ______________________.

She likes to ______________________.

4 Jamie wants to be a ______________________.

He likes to ______________________.

THINK BIG

What's your favorite job in the story? Why?
What do you want to be? Why?

Language in Action

I will listen to a dialog about jobs.

101

8 Listen and read. Then say.

Eddie: I want to be an artist. I like to draw.

Meg: Wow. That's a nice drawing!

Eddie: Thanks. What do you want to be?

Meg: I want to be a vet.

Eddie: Why?

Meg: I really like animals.

Eddie: Animals really like you, too!

9 Look at 8. Role-play with a partner.

102

10 Listen and stick. Then say.

1

2

3

4

Grammar

I will learn to use *want to* + *be* to describe what someone wants to be.

What do you **want to be**?	I **want to be** an actor.
What does he/she **want to be**?	He/She **wants to be** a doctor.

11 Look. Write the answers.

1 What does she want to be?

____

2 What does he want to be?

____

3 What does Sally want to be?

____

4 What does Jim want to be?

____

12 Write.

1 What ______________ he want to be?

2 What ______________ you want to be?

3 What ______________ your cousin want to be?

13 Look at page 56. Point to the people in 1. Ask and answer.

What does he want to be?

He wants to be an actor.

I will learn about goods and services.

14 **Look at the pictures. What are the jobs? How do they help us?**

103

15 **Look , listen, and read. Then circle.**

CONTENT WORDS
carpenter farmer hairdresser
nurse produce provide
server take care of

Goods and Services

Businesses want to make money. There are two ways to do this. They can produce goods, or they can provide services.

1 **Goods** are products. People buy and sell them. Clothes, cars, books, and houses are goods. When a farmer grows food or a carpenter makes a table, they're producing goods.

2 **Services** are activities that people do for others. When a hairdresser cuts your hair or a nurse takes care of you, they're providing a service.

3 Some businesses provide goods and services together. For example, a restaurant sells goods: the food and drink. But it provides services, too. Servers the waiters take the food to the table, and other people wash the dishes after the meal.

1 grow food: **goods / services**

2 cutting hair: **goods / services**

3 a restaurant: **goods / goods and services**

THINK BIG **Do people in these jobs produce goods, provide services, or both?**
pilot artist baker

I will learn about unusual jobs around the world.

16 **Look at the pictures. What kind of jobs are these?**

CONTENT WORDS
bicycle canal customer free lie millions push

Strange Jobs

1 Bicycle Fisher
In Amsterdam, Netherlands, there are many canals. There are also many bicycles. People ride their bikes everywhere. But sometimes people throw their old bikes in the canals. Bicycle Fishers go in the water. They bring the bikes out.

2 Train Pusher
Every morning and evening, millions of people ride the trains around Tokyo, Japan. There are too many people. Not everyone can get on the train. Train pushers help them. They push people inside the trains.

3 Human Bed Warmer
Some hotels in London, in the United Kingdom, pay people to lie in customers' beds. In winter, hotel beds are sometimes cold. Human bed warmers wear special clothes and lie in the beds. The beds get warm.

4 Passenger for Hire
In Jakarta, Indonesia, there are many cars on the road every day. If a driver is alone, he or she must pay money to use the highway. If there are three or more people in the car, the driver does not pay. Some drivers hire people to ride in their car. Then they can drive for free!

105 **17** **Listen and read. Then match with the pictures.**

THINK BIG Which of these jobs would you like to try? Why?

I will learn to use the sounds *ar*, *er*, and *or*.

106 **18** **Listen, look, and repeat.**

1 ar **2** er **3** or

107 **19** **Listen and find. Then say.**

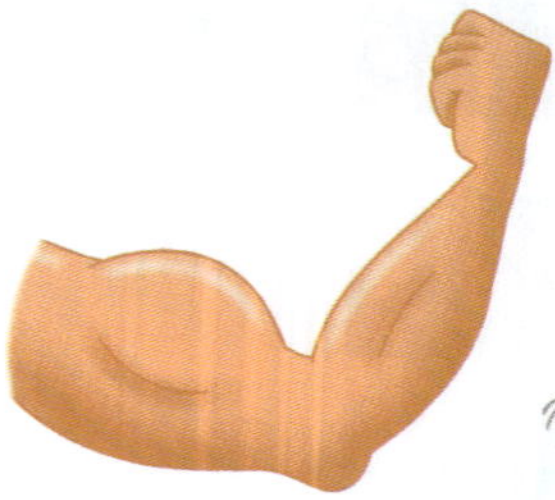

arm

teacher

car

corn

108 **20** **Listen and blend the sounds.**

1 c-ar-t cart
2 s-i-ng-er singer
3 f-or for
4 ar-t art
5 b-or-n born
6 l-e-tt-er letter

109 **21** **Underline ar, er, and or. Then listen and chant.**

I want to be a singer
Or an artist painting art.
I want to be a teacher
Or a farmer with a cart!

I will learn to talk about studying hard and setting goals.

22 Listen and write. Then say.

111

art	math	music	science

1 I like ______________.
I want to be a teacher.

2 I like ______________.
I want to be a doctor.

3 I like ______________.
I want to be a pilot.

4 I like ______________.
I want to be an artist.

THINK BIG

What do you want to be? You like ______________.
What other jobs can you do?

a art **b** music **c** math **d** science

Project

23 Make a What I Want to Be flip book.

1 Paste.

2 Cut.

3 Draw.

4 Show.

24 Look and write.

dancer singer teacher writer

1 ______ 2 ______ 3 ______ 4 ______

25 Read and match.

1 I like to act. I want to be a dancer.
2 I like animals. I want to be a vet.
3 I like to draw. I want to be an actor.
4 I like to move to music. I want to be an artist.

26 Look at the pictures. Write.

1 What does she want to be?

______

because ______.

2 What does he want to be?

______

because ______.

3 What do you want to be?

______

because ______.

I Can

- use job names.

27 **Work in small groups. Ask, "What do you want to be?" Write names and jobs.**

Name	Wants to Be
Raúl	a pilot

28 **Count how many students in 27 want each job. Write a list.**

Job	How Many

29 **Look at this bar chart. Make a bar chart for your group and talk about it.**

One student wants to be a pilot. Three students want to be doctors.

I Can

- say what I want to be and why.
- ask and answer about what people want to be.

6 My Day

Vocabulary

I will learn to name clock times.

112

Song Time!

113

1 Listen, look, and say.

1:00 one o'clock
2:00 two o'clock
3:00 three o'clock
4:00 four o'clock
5:00 five o'clock
6:00 six o'clock
7:00 seven o'clock
8:00 eight o'clock
9:00 nine o'clock
10:00 ten o'clock
11:00 eleven o'clock
12:00 twelve o'clock

2 Play the time game.

Song

I will learn to ask and answer about clock times.

115 116

3 Listen and sing. Then look at 1 and find.

What Time Is It?

Tick, tock. It's seven o'clock.
Time to get up and get dressed.
I want to stay in bed,
But it's time to brush my teeth!

Tick, tock. It's eight o'clock.
At nine o'clock, I start school.
I eat my breakfast and get my books.
I love school, it's cool!

Tick, tock. It's three o'clock.
There's no more school today.
I do my homework, and I go out.
And there's my friend to play.

Now it's evening, and it's eight o'clock,
And it's time to go to bed.
I watch TV and read my book.
Time to sleep now, good night!

117

4 Look at 3. Listen and say yes or no.

5 Look at 1. Ask and answer.

What time is it?

It's one o'clock.

THINK BIG

What time is it now?
What time is it at midday?
What time is it at midnight?

I will read a story about times and daily activities.

119

6 **Listen and read. When does Max get up?**

Max's Day

7 Look at the story. Number in order.

- ☐ Max comes home.
- ☐ Max gets up.
- ☐ Max eats.
- ☐ Max sleeps again.
- ☐ Max goes out.

THINK BIG

What time do you go to bed?
What time do you get up?
How many hours do you sleep?
Is that good or bad?

Language in Action

I will listen to a dialog about times.

120

8 Listen and read. Then say.

Dad: Good morning, Emily. What time is it?

Emily: It's eight o'clock.

Dad: When do you go to school?

Emily: I go to school at eight o'clock.

Dad: So, why are you in your pajamas?

Emily: Oh, Dad! Today's a holiday!

9 Look at 8. Role-play with a partner.

121

10 Listen and stick.

1

2

3

4

Grammar

I will learn to use *when* + the present simple to describe daily activities.

When **does** he/she **get up**?	He/She **gets up** at 6:00.
When **do** you/they **go** to bed?	I/They **go** to bed at 8:00.
When **does** the movie **start**?	It **starts** at 7:00.

11 Look and write do or does.

1 When ________ she brush her teeth?

2 When ________ they eat lunch?

3 When ________ school start?

4 When ________ he go to bed?

5 When ________ school end?

6 When ________ he get up?

12 Look at 11. Write the answers to the questions.

1 She brushes her teeth at 7:00.

2 ________________

3 ________________

4 ________________

5 ________________

6 ________________

I will learn about different ways of telling time.

13 **Look at the pictures. What do all the things do?**

14 **Look, listen, and read. Then match with the pictures.**

CONTENT WORDS
burn candle cup fall
height hourglass
sand shadow sundial

Telling the Time

What time is it? How do you know? Today we look at clocks, watches, and cell phones, but here are some other ways to tell the time. Some are very old.

1 A sundial uses the sun to tell the time. The sun makes a shadow on the sundial, and the shadow tells the time.

2 A candle clock uses a candle to tell the time. When the candle burns, it gets shorter. The height of the candle tells you the time.

3 An hourglass uses sand to tell the time. Sand falls from the top to the bottom. Some people use small hourglasses today when they're cooking.

4 A water clock uses water to tell the time. It works like an hourglass. It has two cups. The water falls from one cup to the other.

THINK BIG Look, think, and draw.

I will learn about different jobs around the world.

CONTENT WORDS
bakery bread fresh market store

a.m. = midnight to noon
p.m. = noon to midnight

125 15 **Listen and read. Write the times.**

Different Jobs, Different Times

I'm Min-jung. My family works at Namdaemun Market in Seoul, South Korea. This market is very big. You can buy anything! My mom and dad have a store here. They sell clothes. Our store opens at ________ p.m. and closes at ________ p.m. Many people shop at night.

I'm Bruno. My sister works at a bakery in São Paulo, Brazil. She gets up at ________ a.m. every day. She goes to work, and she makes bread. Many people like to eat fresh bread in the morning. I like pão de queijo. It's bread with cheese inside.

My name is Sam. My uncle is a pilot. He flies small airplanes in Alaska, in the United States. He gets up at ________ a.m. He takes people, food, or mail to many places. Some days he comes home at ________ p.m. Other days, he comes home at ________ p.m. His work is different every day.

THINK BIG Which job do you like? Why?

I will learn to use the sounds *ch*, *tch*, and *sh*.

126
16 Listen, look, and repeat.

1 ch 2 tch 3 sh

127
17 Listen and find. Then say.

witch

ship

fish

chin

rich

128
18 Listen and blend the sounds.

1	ch-o-p	chop	2	sh-e	she
3	m-a-tch	match	4	l-u-n-ch	lunch
5	d-i-sh	dish	6	w-a-tch	watch

129
19 Underline ch, tch, and sh. Then listen and chant.

Watch the witch,
She's having lunch!
Fries and fish
From a dish!

Values | Be on time.

I will learn to talk about being on time.

131

20 Listen and number in order. Then say.

a

I get dressed quickly and eat breakfast.

b

I always get to school on time.

c

I get my backpack ready the night before school.

d

I get up early on school days.

THINK BIG How do you get to school on time? Why is it good to be on time for school?

Project

21 Make a My Day book.

1 Fold.

2 Draw clocks.

3 Draw what you do.

4 Show your book.

22 Look and write. What time is it?

1 It's ______________. 2 It's ______________. 3 It's ______________.

4 It's ______________. 5 It's ______________. 6 It's ______________.

23 Circle.

1 When **do** / **does** he eat breakfast?

2 When **do** / **does** they get home from school?

3 When **do** / **does** the school bus come?

4 When **do** / **does** you go to bed?

24 Write.

1 What do you do at eight o'clock in the morning?

____

2 What do you do at four o'clock in the afternoon?

____

3 What do you do at nine o'clock at night?

____

I Can

- use *o'clock* to tell the time.
- use the present simple to describe activities.

25 **Play the Silly Sentences game.**

First, write times on cards. Then write daily activities on other cards.

Now work in groups. Stack the cards. Take turns. Turn over one card from each stack, and read a silly sentence.

I Can

- talk about my daily routine with time expressions.
- ask and answer about daily routine activities.

Do I know it?

1 Think about it. Look and circle. Practice.

I know this.

I need more practice.

I don't know this.

1 p. 44

2 p. 56

3 p. 68

4 p. 73

5	He wants to buy a book.	p. 49
6	Is there a movie theater near here? Yes, there is./No, there isn't.	p. 49
7	What do you want to be? I want to be a pilot.	p. 61
8	When does she get up? She gets up at 6:00.	p. 73

Have students review the key language. Go to the pages indicated in each box.

1 2 3 4 5 6 7 8 9

I can do it!

132

2 Get ready.

A. Look, listen, and write.

artist   athlete   do   does   teacher   where

Charlie: Hey, Linda, what do you want to be?

Linda: I want to be an [1] ______________ because I love sports.

Charlie: Really? What [2] ______________ your sister want to be?

Linda: She wants to be an [3] ______________.

Charlie: Why?

Linda: Well, my uncle is an artist. It's his job.

Charlie: [4] ______________ does he work?

Linda: He works at home. He draws pictures for books. What [5] ______________ you want to be, Charlie?

Charlie: I want to be a [6] ______________ because I like school!

B. Talk about what you want to be. Say why.

What do you want to be?

I want to be a vet.
I like animals.

3 Get set.

STEP 1 Cut out the cards on page 135.

STEP 2 Put the cards on your desk. Mix the cards up. Now you're ready to **Go**!

4 Go!

A. Take turns with a partner. Pick up a card. Continue until you find a matching card. Read your cards aloud.

I want to buy a book.

Is there a bookstore near here?

B. Hold up one card at a time and find it on the map. Ask and answer.

Where's the bookstore?

It's on Main Street.

5 Write or draw.

All About Me

What do you want to be? Why?	What time do you start school?
Where's your school?	When do you go to bed?

Do I know it now?

6 Think about it.

A. Go to page 80. Look and circle again.

B. Check (✔).

- ☐ I can start the next unit.
- ☐ I can ask my teacher for help and then start the next unit.
- ☐ I can practice and then start the next unit.

7 Rate this Checkpoint. Color.

hard OK easy | not fun OK fun

1 2 3 4 5 6 7 8 9

7 My Favorite Food

Vocabulary

I will learn to name food.

133

Song Time!

134

1 **Listen, look, and say.**

1 bananas

2 apples

3 strawberries

4 mangoes

5 tomatoes

6 carrots

7 potatoes

8 chicken

9 spaghetti

10 cheese

11 yogurt

12 lemonade

2 **Play the memory game.**

Song

I will learn to ask and answer about food.

135 136

3 Listen and sing. Then look at 1 and find.

Let's Eat Lunch!

It's twelve o'clock.
Let's eat lunch!
I have some bananas.
We can eat a bunch!

Carrots and corn,
Chicken and cheese,
I like them all.
Can I have more, please?

Do you like tomatoes?
I like tomatoes. I really do.
What about potatoes?
I like potatoes, too. Do you?

Have some lemonade
And a sandwich, too.
You and I can share some pie.
I like eating lunch with you.

137

4 Listen, match, and write.

1 I like ______________.

2 I like ______________.

3 I like ______________.

a

b

c

5 Look at 1. Ask and answer.

Do you like bananas?

Yes, I do. I like bananas.

THINK BIG

What do you like to eat for lunch?
What vegetables do you like?

Story

I will read a story about food.

139

6 **Listen and read. Does Dan like apples?**

Do You Like Fruit?

7 Look at the story. Write yes or no.

1 Does Dan like fruit? ____________

2 Does Jamie like bananas? ____________

3 Does Dan like mangoes? ____________

4 Do the boys like pie? ____________

5 Is it a banana pie? ____________

THINK BIG What fruit do you like? When do you like to eat it? What dishes can you make with fruit?

Language in Action

I will listen to a dialog about food.

140

8 **Listen and read. Then say.**

Jeff: I like cheese. May I have two pieces?

Amy: May I have two pieces, too?

Jeff: You always copy me, Amy.

Amy: No, I don't!

Dina: OK, kids. Two for Amy, two for Jeff, and two for me. I like cheese, too!

9 **Look at 8. Role-play with a partner.**

141

10 **Listen and stick.**

1

2

3

4

Grammar

I will learn to use *do/does* + *like* to ask and answer questions about what you like.

Do you **like** fruit?	Yes, I **do**. I like apples and bananas. No, we **don't**. We don't like fruit.
Do they **like** vegetables?	Yes, they **do**. They like carrots and potatoes. No, they **don't**. They like fruit.
Does he/she **like** fruit?	Yes, he/she **does**. He/She likes mangoes and strawberries. No, he/she **doesn't**. He/She likes yogurt.

11 Look. Write.

1 ____________ she ____________ strawberries?

2 ____________ he ____________ tomatoes?

3 ____________ they ____________ corn?

12 Answer the questions in 11. Write.

1 Yes, she does.

2 No, ____________.

3 Yes, ____________. They ____________ vegetables.

13 Look at 11. Ask and answer.

Do you like strawberries?

No, I don't. I like apples.

Content Connection | Science

I will learn about healthy and unhealthy food.

14 **Look at the pictures. Which snacks can you name?**

143

15 **Look, listen, and read. Then circle.**

Healthy and Unhealthy Snacks

Healthy food is good for our body. Some snacks are healthy, but others are not. Unhealthy snacks have too much sugar, fat, or salt.

Sugar

1 Sugar gives us energy, but too much sugar is not healthy. Sugar is bad for our teeth and can make us fatter. Candy has a lot of sugar.

Fat

2 Like sugar, fat gives us energy. When we eat too much of it, it stays in our body and makes us fatter. It is not good for our heart. Chocolate has a lot of fat.

Salt

3 Salt doesn't make us fatter, but too much of it can give us heart disease. Potato chips have a lot of salt.

Many snacks have labels. The labels say how much sugar, fat, and salt is in them. Try to read the labels and choose healthy snacks.

1 candy: a lot of **sugar / salt**
2 chocolate: a lot of **fat / salt**
3 potato chips: a lot of **sugar / salt**

THINK BIG Which snacks in the pictures are healthy? Which are unhealthy?

I will learn about different fruit from around the world.

16 **Look at the pictures. Which fruit do you like to eat?**

CONTENT WORDS
beautiful fabric leaves plants popular tropical ugly

Where Fruit Comes From

Fruit is a very healthy snack. But where does it come from?

1 Watermelons come from South Africa. Turkey, China, and Japan also grow a lot of watermelons. In Japan, they don't only have round watermelons. They have square ones, too!

2 Pineapples grow in tropical countries, such as in South America. There are a lot of pineapple plants in the Philippines, and people there make fabric for clothes from pineapple leaves.

3 Kiwis are China's national fruit! They come from China, but now they grow in many parts of the world, like Italy and New Zealand. Their skin is ugly, but inside they're beautiful.

4 Many avocados come from Mexico, but they're popular all over the world. In Indonesia, people make a sweet drink with avocado, milk, sugar, and sometimes chocolate.

145

17 **Listen and read. Then match.**

1	Pineapples	**a**	South Africa
2	Watermelons	**b**	China
3	Avocados	**c**	South America
4	Kiwis	**d**	Mexico

THINK BIG Supermarkets sell fruit from around the world. How do you know where it comes from?

Phonics | *ee, ie*

I will learn to use the sounds *ee* and *ie*.

146 18 Listen, look, and repeat.

1 ee 2 ie

147 19 Listen and find. Then say.

sheep

pie

bee

tie

148 20 Listen and blend the sounds.

1	f-ee-t	feet
2	l-ie	lie
3	s-ee	see
4	f-l-ie-s	flies
5	ch-ee-se	cheese
6	c-r-ie-d	cried

149 21 Underline ee and ie. Then listen and chant.

"See the cheese!"
Cried the bees.
"See the pies!"
Cried the flies.

Values | Choose healthy foods.

I will learn to talk about choosing healthy foods.

151

22 Listen and number. Then write and say.

apple	carrots	chips	cookie

a

I want an ________, please.

b

No ________, for me, thanks.

c

Just one more ________, please.

d

I like ________.

23 Look at 22. Role-play with a partner.

I want a carrot, please.

No chocolate for me, thanks.

THINK BIG

What healthy food did you eat today?
What unhealthy food did you eat today?

Project

24 Make a Healthy Snacks collage.

1 Cut. 2 Write. 3 Paste. 4 Show.

25 Look and write likes or doesn't like.

1 She ____________ cookies.

2 He ____________ salad.

3 He ____________ milk.

4 He ____________ ice cream.

5 He ____________ bananas.

6 He ____________ pizza.

26 Write.

1 Do you like cheese?

____

2 Do you like pineapples?

____

3 Do you like tomatoes?

____

I Can

- use words for types of foods.
- use *like/likes* or *don't like/doesn't like* with food words.

27 Play the What Do You Like? game.

1 Circle yes for the foods you like. Circle no for the foods you don't like.

2 Guess what your partner likes. Circle.

3 Your partner says what he or she likes. Check (✓) your correct guesses.

		YOU		YOUR PARTNER		CORRECT?
1	carrots	yes	no	yes	no	
2	cheese	yes	no	yes	no	
3	tomatoes	yes	no	yes	no	
4	pineapple	yes	no	yes	no	
5	lemonade	yes	no	yes	no	
6	chicken	yes	no	yes	no	
7	spaghetti	yes	no	yes	no	
8	yogurt	yes	no	yes	no	
9	strawberries	yes	no	yes	no	
10	potatoes	yes	no	yes	no	

Greg, do you like carrots?

Yes, I do.

Greg likes carrots.
He doesn't like cheese.

28 Tell the class what your partner likes and doesn't like.

I Can

- say what food I like and don't like.
- ask and answer about food people like and don't like.

8 Wild Animals

Vocabulary

I will learn to name animals.

152

Song Time!

153

1 Listen, look, and say.

1 giraffe

2 hippo

3 kangaroo

4 cheetah

5 polar bear

6 zebra

7 monkey

8 peacock

9 elephant

10 crocodile

2 Play the acting game.

Song

I will learn to ask and answer about animals.

154 155

3 Listen and sing. Then look at 1 and find.

To the Zoo!

I really like animals!
Do you like them, too?
That's why I'm so happy.
We're going to the zoo!

A kangaroo can jump.
A monkey can jump, too.
Crocodiles can chase
And swim.
And you, what can you do?

A giraffe can't fly or jump up high.
An elephant can't climb trees.
Fish can't run, and hippos can't fly.
Come and see them.
Oh, yes, please!

Now it's time to say goodbye
To every animal here.
But we can come back
And see them every year!

156

4 Listen and say true or false.

5 Look at 1. Ask and answer.

Do you like cheetahs?

Yes, I do!
Cheetahs can run.

THINK BIG

Which animals can chase other animals?
Which animals can climb trees?

I will read a story about animals.

158

6 Listen and read. What animals does Jamie like?

Monkeys Are Great!

7 Look. Circle can or can't.

1 Monkeys **can** / **can't** climb trees.

2 Monkeys **can** / **can't** jump.

3 Hippos **can** / **can't** climb trees.

4 Hippos **can** / **can't** jump.

5 Hippos **can** / **can't** eat a lot.

6 Jamie **can** / **can't** eat a lot.

THINK BIG What animals can swim, run, and eat fish? What animals can't fly or climb trees?

Language in Action

I will listen to a dialog about animals.

159

8 Listen and read. Then say.

Lee: What's that?

Josh: It's a toucan. Look.
It has a big, colorful beak.

Lee: Can it talk?

Josh: Well... no, it can't.
But it can fly.

Lee: Look at the parrot. Parrots are very colorful. They can fly. And they can talk, too!

9 Look at 8. Role-play with a partner.

160

10 Listen and stick. Then write the word.

claws pouch tail trunk

1 ____________________

2 ____________________

3 ____________________

4 ____________________

Grammar

I will learn to use *can/can't* to describe what animals can do.

Can a kangaroo jump?	Yes, it **can**.	**Can** an elephant jump?	No, it **can't**.
Can kangaroos jump?	Yes, they **can**.	**Can** elephants jump?	No, they **can't**.

162

11 Look and listen. Then write.

1 ________ a zebra see at night? Yes, ____________.

2 ________ cheetahs run fast? Yes, ____________.

3 ________ a giraffe climb a tree? No, ____________.

4 ________ hippos jump? No, ____________.

12 Match the questions and answers.

1 Can monkeys hang from trees?

2 Can a lion catch animals for its food?

3 Can elephants climb trees?

a No, they can't. They're too big.

b Yes, they can. They have long tails.

c Yes, it can. It has sharp claws.

13 Look at pages 100–101. Ask and answer with a partner.

Can a monkey hang from a tree?

Yes, it can.

I will learn about where animals live.

14 **Look at the pictures. Which animals can you name?**

163 **15** **Look, listen, and read. Then circle.**

CONTENT WORDS

cover desert forest fox jungle lizard ocean racoon sea whale

Animal Habitats

A habitat is the place where an animal lives.

The **forest** is a cool, dark habitat with a lot of trees. Deer, raccoons, and foxes live there. Forests cover 1 **8% / 28%** of the planet.

2 **6% / 60%** of our planet is **desert**. It's hot in the day and cold at night. There isn't much rain, so it's very dry, and there aren't many plants. Lizards and snakes live there.

The **ocean** covers 3 **21% / 71%** of our planet, and the water in it is salty. Many kinds of fish live in the ocean. Other animals live there, too, like whales and seals.

It's hot in the **jungle**, and it rains a lot. Monkeys, colorful birds, and butterflies live there. There are tigers, too! The jungle covers only 4 **2% / 12%** of the planet, but 50% of all plant and animal species live there.

THINK BIG Which animal habitats are in your country? Which animals live there?

I will learn about helping animals around the world.

165 16 **Look, listen, and read. Then match and write 1–3.**

They live on a farm. ☐ They live in the jungle. ☐ They live in a camp. ☐

People Helping Animals

Do you like animals? Around the world, people are helping animals.

1

Helping Elephants in Myanmar

In Myanmar, you can visit old elephants. These elephants work for a long time. They help carry trees. When they are old, they can't work. Some come to a special camp. You can visit the elephants here. You can feed them and give them a bath.

2

Helping Horses in Canada

In Canada, some people help horses. These horses are sometimes old. Some are sick or hurt. Some don't have a home. At special farms, the horses can live in a clean, safe place. Vets come and take care of them.

3

Helping Chimpanzees in Kenya

In Kenya, you can see chimpanzees at a special place in the jungle. Some of the animals come here because they don't have a mother or father. Others are hurt. The chimpanzees have a good home here. People can visit and learn more about them.

THINK BIG What other kinds of animals need help from people?

I will learn to use the sounds *ou* and *ow*.

166 17 Listen, look, and repeat.

1 ou   2 ow

167 18 Listen and find. Then say.

cow

soup

owl

you

168 19 Listen and blend the sounds.

1	g-r-ou-p	group	2	t-ow-n	town
3	t-ou-c-a-n	toucan	4	c-l-ow-n	clown
5	d-ow-n	down	6	s-ou-p	soup

169 20 Underline ou and ow. Then listen and chant.

An owl went
Down to town
To see a group
Of toucans
Drinking soup.

Values | Appreciate animals.

I will learn to talk about appreciating animals.

171 21 Listen and number. Then say.

a

I think peacocks are beautiful.

b

Monkeys are so smart.

c

Giraffes are amazing. Their necks are so long.

d

Elephants are very strong.

22 Look at 21. Ask and answer.

What animal do you like?

I like peacocks. They're so beautiful.

THINK BIG What is your favorite animal? Why?

Project

23 Make an Animals Map of your country.

1 Draw a map.

2 Color the habitats.

3 Cut out pictures.

4 Paste the pictures.

24 Look and write.

1 Can a ________ swim?
Yes, ________.

2 Can a ________ fly?
No, ________.

3 Can an ________ talk?
No, ________.

4 Can a ________ jump?
Yes, ________.

25 Number the conversation in order.

☐ Yes, it can.
☐ Yes, I like its tail. Can it fly?
☐ It's a peacock.
☐ Hey, Patrick. What's that?
☐ Wow. It's beautiful!
☐ Yes, it is. It has a big, colorful tail.

I Can

- use words for wild animals.
- use *can/can't* with action words.

26 Play the What Animal Am I? game.

Step 1. Write the name of an animal on a sticky note. Don't show your partner.

Step 2. Stick your note on your partner's forehead. Your partner asks you questions and guesses the animal.

Step 3. Now play with other partners.

I Can

- ask and answer questions about what animals can do.

9 Fun All Year

Vocabulary

I will learn to name the months of the year.

173 Song Time!

174 **1** Listen, look, and say.

January

SUN	MON	TUE	WED	THU	FRI	SAT
1	2	3	4	5	6	7
8	9	10	11	12	13	14
15	16	17	18	19	20	21
22	23	24	25	26	27	28
29	30	31				

February

SUN	MON	TUE	WED	THU	FRI	SAT
			1	2	3	4
5	6	7	8	9	10	11
12	13	14	15	16	17	18
19	20	21	22	23	24	25
26	27	28	29			

March

SUN	MON	TUE	WED	THU	FRI	SAT
				1	2	3
4	5	6	7	8	9	10
11	12	13	14	15	16	17
18	19	20	21	22	23	24
25	26	27	28	29	30	31

April

SUN	MON	TUE	WED	THU	FRI	SAT
1	2	3	4	5	6	7
8	9	10	11	12	13	14
15	16	17	18	19	20	21
22	23	24	25	26	27	28
29	30					

May

SUN	MON	TUE	WED	THU	FRI	SAT
		1	2	3	4	5
6	7	8	9	10	11	12
13	14	15	16	17	18	19
20	21	22	23	24	25	26
27	28	29	30	31		

June

SUN	MON	TUE	WED	THU	FRI	SAT
					1	2
3	4	5	6	7	8	9
10	11	12	13	14	15	16
17	18	19	20	21	22	23
24	25	26	27	28	29	30

July

SUN	MON	TUE	WED	THU	FRI	SAT
1	2	3	4	5	6	7
8	9	10	11	12	13	14
15	16	17	18	19	20	21
22	23	24	25	26	27	28
29	30	31				

August

SUN	MON	TUE	WED	THU	FRI	SAT
			1	2	3	4
5	6	7	8	9	10	11
12	13	14	15	16	17	18
19	20	21	22	23	24	25
26	27	28	29	30	31	

September

SUN	MON	TUE	WED	THU	FRI	SAT
						1
2	3	4	5	6	7	8
9	10	11	12	13	14	15
16	17	18	19	20	21	22
23	24	25	26	27	28	29
30						

October

SUN	MON	TUE	WED	THU	FRI	SAT
	1	2	3	4	5	6
7	8	9	10	11	12	13
14	15	16	17	18	19	20
21	22	23	24	25	26	27
28	29	30	31			

November

SUN	MON	TUE	WED	THU	FRI	SAT
				1	2	3
4	5	6	7	8	9	10
11	12	13	14	15	16	17
18	19	20	21	22	23	24
25	26	27	28	29	30	

December

SUN	MON	TUE	WED	THU	FRI	SAT
						1
2	3	4	5	6	7	8
9	10	11	12	13	14	15
16	17	18	19	20	21	22
23	24	25	26	27	28	29
30	31					

2 Play the ordering game.

Song

I will learn to ask and answer about months.

175 176

3 Listen and sing. Then look at 1 and find.

I Like July!

July is my favorite month.
I like August, too.
I'm happy and on vacation,
There is so much to do!

I also like September.
That's when I start school.
I'm so excited, aren't you?
My friends will be there, too!

I don't like December.
It's very, very cold.
But then it is my birthday, too.
This year, I'm eight years old!

177

4 Listen and write the month.

1 ______ 2 ______ 3 ______

5 Look at 1. Ask and answer.

What's your favorite month?

I like May.

THINK BIG Which months do you have vacation?

Story

I will read a story about what people do during each month.

179 **6** **Listen and read. When is Jamie's birthday?**

Fun in August!

7 Look at the story. Circle.

1 Jenny's favorite month is **January** / **December**.

2 Dan goes swimming in **January** / **August**.

3 Jamie's favorite month is **August** / **May**.

4 Jenny always goes on vacation in **December** / **November**.

5 Dan never goes on vacation in **August** / **December**.

6 Jamie always has a party in **April** / **August**.

THINK BIG

When do you go on vacation?
I always go on vacation in ______________.
I never go on vacation in ______________.

Language in Action

I will listen to a dialog about special days.

180 8 Listen and read. Then say.

Ted: Is Mother's Day always in May and Father's Day in June? Is there a Children's Day?

Dad: Yes, many families celebrate mothers in May and fathers in June. Some families celebrate children in November.

Ted: We never celebrate Children's Day.

Mom: Let's celebrate this year. What do you want to do?

Ted: Let's have a party and invite all our cousins and friends.

Tina: Cool! We can play games and eat our favorite foods!

9 Look at 8. Role-play with a partner.

181 10 Listen and stick. Then write the number.

a

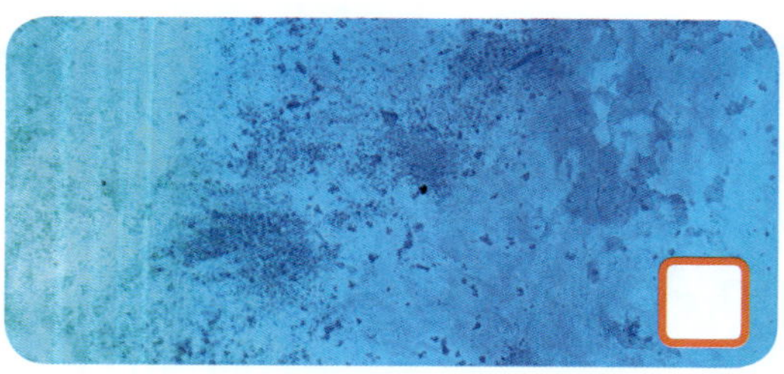

We always swim in the ocean.

b

We always go to my grandpa's house.

c

We always go on vacation.

d

I always play soccer with my friends.

Grammar

I will learn to use *always* and *never* to describe what we do during each season.

What does he/she do in January?	He/She **always** has a New Year's party in January.
What do they do in the spring?	They **always** play baseball in the park.
Do you go on vacation in the winter?	No, I/we don't. I/We **never** go on vacation in the winter.

11 Write always or never.

1 What do they do in the summer? Do they go on vacation?
Yes, they ______________ go on vacation in the summer.

2 Do you go to the beach in the winter?
No, we don't. We ______________ go to the beach in the winter.

3 What does she do on Mother's Day?
She ______________ gives her mother a present.

12 Read. Complete the dialog.

always Do never What

Gina: ______________ do you do in the summer?

Billy: We go to the beach in the summer.
Do you go to the beach, too?

Gina: No, we ______________ go to the beach.
We always go to the mountains.

Billy: ______________ you go with your family?

Gina: Yes, I ______________ go with my family.

13 Ask and answer. Use always and never.

1 What do you do in the winter?

2 Do you go to school in the summer?

Content Connection | Geography

I will learn about seasonal celebrations.

14 **Look at pictures a–d. What are the people doing?**

183

15 **Look, listen, and read. When are the festivals? Number in order from January.**

CONTENT WORDS

celebration confetti hang mask pole ribbon wish

Celebrating Special Days

Every country has special days and exciting celebrations. Let's take a look at some of them.

People in England celebrate spring on May 1st. On May Day, people put flowers and ribbons on a special pole. Children hold the ribbons and dance around the pole.

Italy is famous for its carnivals. In February and March, there are parties in the streets. People wear masks, and the children throw small pieces of paper called confetti.

In China, people celebrate the Mid-Autumn Festival. This festival happens in September or October when the moon is very big and bright. Children wear colorful masks and dance in the streets. They also eat sweet cakes called mooncakes.

In Japan, people celebrate the star festival, Tanabata. In July and August, people write wishes on paper. They hang the wishes on bamboo to make a "wish tree."

- ☐ May Day
- ☐ Mid-Autumn Festival
- ☐ Carnivals in Italy
- ☐ Tanabata

THINK BIG What celebrations does your country have? What do people do?

I will learn about how people celebrate New Year's Eve around the world.

185

16 Look, listen, and read. Why are the foods special?

CONTENT WORDS
bell chime coal luck ring

New Year's Eve

People all over the world celebrate New Year's Eve on the night of December 31st. It's the last day of the year, and there are a lot of parties. But celebrations at midnight are very different in different places.

In Spain, people eat twelve grapes at twelve o'clock – one with every chime of the clock. People think that the grapes bring good luck for the next year. Then there are fireworks.

In Scotland, New Year's Eve is called Hogmanay. At midnight, people hold hands and sing a special song about old friends. Then they visit their friends' and family's homes. The first person through the door gives a piece of coal to bring good luck to the family.

In Japan, people eat a special noodle soup on New Year's Eve for good luck. They eat the soup and listen to a bell ring 108 times at midnight. They believe the bell takes away 108 bad things before the New Year.

17 Look at 16. Match.

1 Spain
2 Scotland
3 Japan

a listen to something
b sing a song
c eat fruit

THINK BIG What do people in your country do when they want good luck? Do you think it works?

I will learn to use the alphabet.

186 18 **Listen, look, and say.**

Aa	Bb	Cc	Dd	Ee	
Ff	Gg	Hh	Ii	Jj	
Kk	Ll	Mm	Nn	Oo	
Pp	Qq	Rr	Ss	Tt	
Uu	Vv	Ww	Xx	Yy	Zz

187 19 **Listen, look, and chant. Can you find something starting with every letter of the alphabet?**

A, B, C, D, E, F, G.
I can see an ant and a bat. What can you see?
H, I, J, K, L, M, N, O, P.
I can see a lion and some ink. What can you see?
Q, R, S, T, U, V.
I can see a rat and a snake. What can you see?
W, X, Y, and Z.
Six yellow wolves and a zebra are what I see!

Values | Be active all year.

I will learn to talk about being active all year.

189

20 Listen and write the season. Then say.

fall   spring   winter   summer

1

In the ________, they skate on ice.

2

In the ________, he rides his bike.

3

In the ________, she likes to swim.

4

In the ________, they rake leaves.

THINK BIG What can you only do in the winter? Why? What can you only do in the summer? Why?

Project

21 Make a Special Days calendar.

22 Look and match.

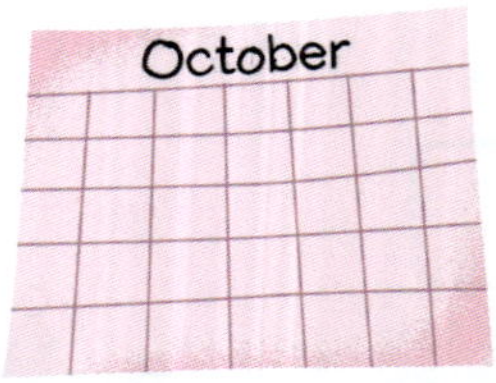

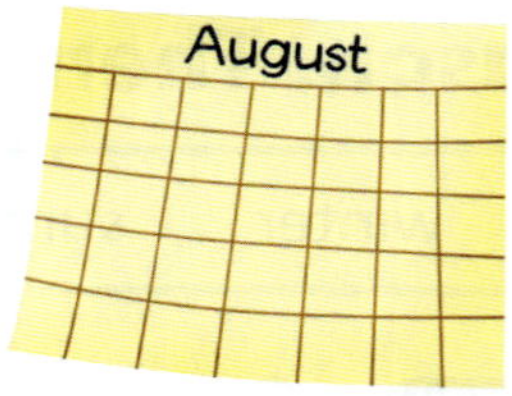

a 

b 

c 

d 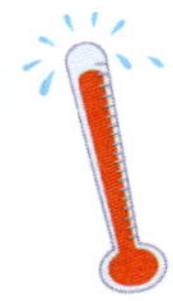

23 Write about you.

1 What do you do in the winter?

I always ______________________ in the winter.

I never ______________________ in the winter.

2 What do you do in the summer?

I always ______________________ in the summer.

I never ______________________ in the summer.

3 What do you do in the fall?

I always ______________________ in the fall.

I never ______________________ in the fall.

4 What do you do in the spring?

I always ______________________ in the spring.

I never ______________________ in the spring.

I Can

- use words for months, seasons, and celebrations.
- use *always* or *never* to describe regular activities.

24 Play the **Months Lineup** game.

Step 1. Ask when your classmates' birthdays are. Then line up in order by month.

Step 2. Check the order with the class.

Step 3. Play the game again. Ask and answer. Then line up again by month.

1. What is your favorite month?
2. What is your favorite holiday?
3. When is your favorite school event?

I Can

- talk about important activities and events that happen in a year.
- ask and answer questions about what people do at different times in a year.

Checkpoint | Units 7–9

Do I know it?

1 Think about it. Look and circle. Practice.

I know this.

I need more practice.

I don't know this.

1 p. 84

2 p. 96

3 p. 100

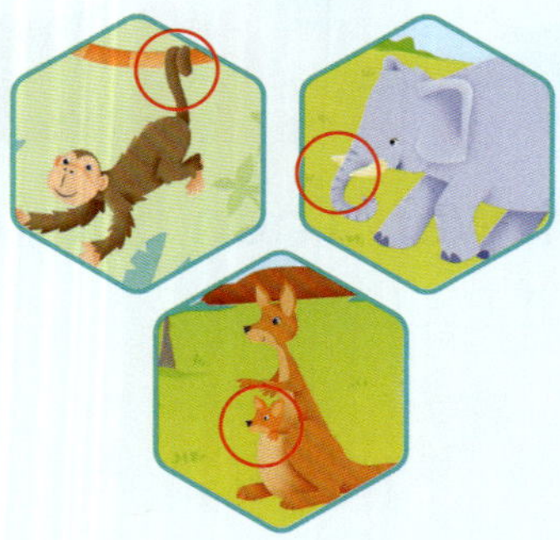

4 p. 108

5	Does she like fruit? Yes, she does./No, she doesn't.		p. 89
6	Can elephants jump? Yes, they can./No, they can't.		p. 101
7	What does he do in January? He always has a New Year's party in January.		p. 113
8	Do you go on vacation in the winter? Yes, we do./No, we don't.		p. 113

Have students review the key language. Go to the pages indicated in each box.

I can do it!

190

2 Get ready.

A. Look, listen, and write.

always can can't never

Alan: Is that your parrot? He's so colorful!

Tess: Yes. His name is Crackers. He's a smart bird. He [1]__________ talk!

Alan: He can?

Tess: Yes. Listen. Crackers – are you a pretty bird?

Crackers: Yes. I'm a pretty bird.

Alan: That's cool! What does he eat?

Tess: Oh, he likes to eat bananas, carrots, and apples.

Crackers: Crackers wants an apple.

Alan: Wow!

Tess: He can sing "Happy Birthday," too.

Alan: Really?

Tess: Yes. He [2]__________ sings to me on my birthday.

Alan: Wow. My cat is so boring. She [3]__________ say anything, and she [4]__________ sings to me!

B. Look at **A**. Ask and answer.

What can Crackers do?

He can talk and sing.

What are two things Crackers can say?

1 2 3 4 5 6 7 8 9

3 Get set.

STEP 1 Cut out the outline on page 137. Cut each card in half along the dotted line.

STEP 2 Sort the cards into two piles. Put the heads of the animals in one pile and the bodies in the other. Now you're ready to **Go**!

4 Go!

A. Put one card from each of your piles together to make a funny animal.

B. Talk about your funny animals. Ask and answer.

What does your animal look like?

My animal has a long trunk and stripes.

What do you call your animal?

I call my animal an elebra.

C. Look at others' animals. Who has the same animal as you?

5 Write or draw.

All About Me

When is your birthday?	What do you like to eat on your birthday?
What's your favorite month?	What do you always do in the summer?

Do I know it now?

6 Think about it.

A. Go to page 120. Look and circle again.

B. Check (✔).

☐ I can ask my teacher for help.

☐ I can practice.

7 Rate this Checkpoint. Color.

hard OK easy | not fun OK fun

– 5 questions –

191

Look at the pictures. Now listen and look. There is one example.

What's Alex doing?

A ☐

B ☑

C ☐

1 What's Jill doing?

A ☐

B ☐

C ☐

2 What's Ben doing?

A ☐

B ☐

C ☐

3 Where is Pat's jacket?

A ☐

B ☐

C ☐

4 How many people are in the picture?

A ☐

B ☐

C ☐

5 What are Bill and Ann doing?

A ☐

B ☐

C ☐

– 5 questions –

192

Look at the picture. Listen and write a name or a number. There are two examples.

Examples

What is the boy's name? Tom

How old is he? 10

Questions

1 How old is Sara? ____________________

2 How many books does Tom have? ____________________

3 What's the name of the cat? ____________________

4 What's the name of the dog? ____________________

5 Where's the library? on __________ Street

– 5 questions –

Look and read. Put a check (✓) or an (✗) in the box. There are two examples.

Examples

She is a doctor. ✓

This is a bus stop. ✗

Questions

1

This is a bookstore. ☐

2

She is a dancer. ☐

3

He is a mail carrier. ☐

4

This is a gas station. ☐

5

He is a singer. ☐

– 5 questions –

Look at the pictures. Look at the letters. Write the words.

Example

s w i n g — gwins

Questions

1

_ _ _ _ _ _ _ _ — retmocup

2

_ _ _ _ _ — desli

3

_ _ _ _ _ _ _ _ _ _ — taskedrabo

4

_ _ _ _ _ _ — neclip

5

_ _ _ _ _ _ _ — reticup

– 5 questions –

Read. Choose a word from the box. Write the correct word next to numbers 1–5. There is one example.

Zoos are big places. A lot of animals live there. The elephant has big ears and a long trunk. The (1) ____________ is a bird with a beautiful tail. The (2) ____________ is another beautiful bird. It likes to talk. Then there are (3) ____________. They have long tails and live in trees. The (4) ____________ is a large, gray animal with small ears. It likes the water. And the (5) ____________ has a long neck and spots.

Example 			

Joe's Coffee Shop
BUS STOP
Post Office

Cutouts for Page 42, Checkpoint Units 1–3

We want to go to the post office.	**Is there a post office near here?**
I want to buy a book.	**Is there a bookstore near here?**
My mom wants to eat lunch.	**Is there a restaurant near here?**
My grandma wants to buy cookies and milk.	**Is there a supermarket near here?**
My dad wants to put gas in the car.	**Is there a gas station near here?**

Pearson Education Limited
KAO Two
KAO Park
Harlow
Essex
CM17 9NA
England
and Associated Companies throughout the world.

www.pearsonenglish.com/bigenglish2

Authorised adaptation from the United States edition entitled Big English, 1st Edition, by Mario Herrera and Christopher Sol Cruz. Published by Pearson Education Inc. © 2013 by Pearson Education, Inc.

First published 2021
Second impression 2023
ISBN: 978-1-2923-9269-1

Set in Heinemann Roman
Printed in Slovakia by Neografia

Acknowledgements

Picture Credits
The publisher would like to thank the following for their kind permission to reproduce their photographs:

(Key: b-bottom; c-centre; l-left; r-right; t-top)

123RF.com: Ian Allenden 65tr, captblack76 114 (b), Dolgachov 4/6, 15b (watching), 40tl (watching), Patrick Hastings 115tl, Jreika 115tr, Vera Kuttelvaserova Stuchelova Intro c/4, Max Lashcheuski 88 (cheese), lsaloni 115tc, Maxaltamor 34 (a), Gilberto Mevi 90br, Neven Milinkovi 51 (d), Nyul Intro c/2, Sergein 60/4, Spectral Intro c/5, Kladej Voravongsuk 8tl, Wavebreak Media Ltd 4/4, 14/1, 14b (glue), 21c, Nataliia Zhekova 94/6, 95b (pizza); **Alamy Stock Photo:** Aflo Co. Ltd 114 (d), Asia Images Group Pte Ltd 55cr, 57bl, 85cr, AsiaDreamPhoto 63 (b), Bamboofox 114 (c), Jeffrey Blackler 44/1, 80tl (movie theatre), Blend Images 56/6, 66b (pilot), Joerg Boethling 35/2, Ron Bull 74 (d), Cultura Creative 94/1, Cultura Creative (RF) 11/1, Denkou Images 67t, Chad Ehlers 63 (d), Glow Asia RF Stickers 2 (pilot), Greatstock / Alamy Stock Photo 13b, Hemis 50 (d), Cindy Hopkins 103/1, imageBROKER 51 (b), IMAGEMORE Co., Ltd 54c, incamerastock 54t/2, Johner Images 114 (a), Ton Koene 63 (c), Alistair Laming 74 (b), Bruce Leighty 54t/3, Bob Masters 34 (d), Patti McConville 44/6, Graham Oliver 44/11, Pawel Libera Images 34 (b), Mariusz Prusaczyk 75tl, Juergen Ritterbach 103/3, Alex Segre 44/7, 51 (c), 54b (bookstore), Simon Margetson Travel 28br, 38b (bedroom), 40bl (bedroom), TomBham 44/5, 55b (bus stop), Westend61 GmbH / Alamy Stock Photo 109b/2, 119cr, Gari Wyn Williams 54t/1, YAY Media AS / Alamy Stock Photo 88; **Fotolia.com:** 38/1, 39b (oven), Abdue 28tr, 38b (bathroom), Africa Studio 9b (cake), 14b (cake), Akulamatiau 60/3, Aussieanouk 105 (b), Andrey Bandurenko 29tr, 39b (chair), Sergiy Bykhunenko 16/6, 26/2, 26b (skate), 40tr (skating), Claireliz 45tl, Dasharosato 50 (c), Dazb75 9 (dog), 14b (dog), Dimitrius 49t, George Dolgikh 66c (artist), f9photos 74 (a), Famveldman 4/3, 15b (cutting), 40tl (cutting), Goodluz 56/5, 66t (writer), GoodMood Photo 38/3, Gpointstudio 9/4, 14/6, Igorphoto50 84/12, 120tl (lemonade), Ilike 4/2, 14b (counting), 94/2, 95/2, Michael Ireland 25cr, Alexandra Karamyshev 39 (hat), Dusan Kostic 9/1, 14/4, Jakub Krechowicz 84/7, Krsmanovic 44/3, 80tl (restaurant), Pavel Losevsky 44/10, 54b (shopping mall), Lucky Dragon 25l, Matka_Wariatka 5t, Monkey Business 25cl, 112t, Moodboard 117/3, 118cr, Morenovel 11/2, Motorlka 84/6, 85br, 120tl (carrots), Sergey Novikov 16/2, 20, 26b (volleyball), Tyler Olson 56/11, 80tr (vet), Alena Ozerova 32, Pololia 16/1, 27b (basketball), 40tr (basketball), Andrey Popov 62br, Giuseppe Porzani 44/2, 55b (gas station), 80tl (gas station), r-o-x-o-r 50 (a), Rido 60t, Andres Rodriguez 109b/1, 119cl, Olga Sapegina 85t, Shock 44/8, Shutswis 38/4, Snaptitude Stickers 2 (dancer), StockPhotosArt 39 (roller skates), Sumnersgraphicsinc 39 (soccer ball), Sveta 39 (glasses), 39b (glasses), Tammykayphoto 16/3, 26/4, 26b (baseball), Twixx 39 (keys), 39b (keys), Valizal4 94/4, Tom Wang Stickers 2 (sing), WavebreakmediaMicro 9/2, 9/3, 14/2, 14/3, Monika Wisniewska 65br, yanlev 16/7, Joanna Zielinska Intro c/3; **Getty Images:** Valentin Casarsa 23b, Jonas Gratzer / LightRocket 11/4, IMAGEMORE Co., Ltd. 23c, Kali9 11/3, MIXA 112 (c), Martin Puddy 35/4, Rubberball / Mike Kemp 108, 118cl, Damir Spanic 56/1, Kazumasa Yanai 29cl, 60/2; **Imagestate Media:** John Foxx Collection 112 (d); **Pearson Education Ltd:** Studio 8 15cr, 49bl, 57br, 82tl, 93br, 97br, Gareth Boden 103/2, Trevor Clifford 10br, Welcome Page dbl, Welcome Page dbr, Naki Kouyioumtzis 44/4, 55b (train station), Tudor Photography 21b, Jules Selmes 4/8, 4/9, 15b (writing), 56/10, 66b (chef), Stickers 2 (chef); **Shutterstock.com:** Africa Studio 91br, Andrjuss 84/10, Andy Dean Photography 56/4, Apples Eyes Studio 65tl, Artjazz. S 66t (dancer), Nick Berrisford 102tl, Dean Bertoncelj 62cl, Ruth Black 10c, Andre Blais 16/4, 25r, 26/1, 27b (slide), 40tr (slide), Blend Images 57t, BlueRingMedia 22br, Mark Bonham 56/3, 66b (dancer), 80tr (ballerina), Willyam Bradberry 102br, CandyBox Images Intro c/6, Cdrin 75bl, Steve Cukrov 66c (doctor), Davegkugler 96/1, 105 (c), 106/2, 120tr (giraffe), Eurobanks 90tr, Iakov Filimonov 96/5, 106/1, Chris Fourie 97tl, Stephanie Frey 37t, Goodluz 62tr, Alexey Goosev 96/6, 106b (zebra), 120tr (zebra), Skazka Grez 90bl, Shawn Hempel 105 (a), Jiri Hera 90tl, Holbox 100, Chris Howey 51 (a), Hurst Photo 4/5, IB Photography 14c (marker pen), Idiz 96/3, 106/4, 120tr (kangaroo), Christopher Jones 56/2, 80tr (artist), John Kasawa 29cr, 38/6, Kesu 112 (b), Kinga 48, 54b (talking), Kkammphoto008 35/3, Serhiy Kobyakov 4/1, 14/5, 15b (colouring), 40tl (drawing), Vladimir Koletic 56/7, 66b (singer), Vitaly Korovin 84/5, Kzenon 22bl, Ledoct 66t (singer), Henrik Lehnerer 102bl, LightField Studios 72, Lynnette 38/2, Robyn Mackenzie 9b (shapes), Bruce MacQueen 102tr, Viktar Malyshchyts 84/1, 91tr, Rob Marmion 16/5, 22tr, 26/3, 27b (soccer), MaxyM Intro c/7, Mexrix 84/11, 85bl, Monkey Business Images 4/7, 15cl, 29bl, 29br, 33bl, 37b, 39cl, 39cr, 45bl, 45br, 50bl, 50br, 61bl, 61br, 66t (teacher), 69bl, 69br, 81bl, 81br, 82bl, 82br, 85c, 89br, 93bl, 94/3, 97bl, Nate A 109c, 119l, Dmitry Naumov 16/8, 27b (ride bike), 117/2, Naypong 96/10, 106b (crocodile), Carlos Neto 96/2, odze 84/3, 85bc, 120tl (strawberries), Presniakov Oleksandr 74 (c), Krishna Utkarsh Pandit 105 (d), Csaba Peterdi 117/1, 118l, Photographee.eu 28tl, 38b (living room), 40bl (living room), 94/5, 95b (banana), Stu Porter 96/4, Rickyd 96/8, 106c, 106b (peacock), riekephotos 37c, Eduardo Rivero 96/7, 106b (monkey), Karen Roach 14c (rulers), Robcartorres 63 (a), Rocharibeiro 75cr, rzymuR 39 (phone), SergiyN 5br, 10bl, 11br, 13tl, 17br, 49br, 67b, 82tr, 85cl, 95tl, 101bl, Intro cbl, Intro cbr, Rohit Seth 8tr, 60/1, Dmitriy Shironosov 56/9, Iriana Shiyan 28bl, 38b (kitchen), 40bl (kitchen), Victor Shova 96/9, 106/3, Sixninepixels 38/5, Slaven 65bl, Smit 68, 69c, 78, Bryan Solomon 90cl, Alex Staroseltsev 91bl, James Steidl 34 (c), Michaela Stejskalova 84/9, 94b (spaghetti), Margaret M Stewart 14c (eraser), Sirikorn Thamniyom 21t, Leah-Anne Thompson 109t, Tods 50 (b), Tungphoto 29tl, Dani Vincek 84/8, Visionsi 56/8, Valentyn Volkov 84/4, 91tl, Tatyana Vyc 84/2, 94b (apples), Wavebreakmedia 23t, worldswildlifewonders 97tr, XiXinXing 117/4, 118r, Senol Yaman 112 (a), Lisa F. Young Intro c/1, Zigroup-Creations 35/1, Zimmytws 22tl; **SuperStock:** Blend Images 5bl, 11bl, 17bl, 33br, 55cl, 89bl, 95tr, 101br, Corbis 109b/3, 119r; **www.imagesource.com:**
Cover images: *Front:* **Getty Images:** strmko

All other images © Pearson Education

Illustrated by
Robin Boyer, Martyn Cain, Andrew Hennessey, Zaharias Papadopoulos, Jose Rubio, Christos Skaltsas, Julia Wolf.